W9-BLH-605

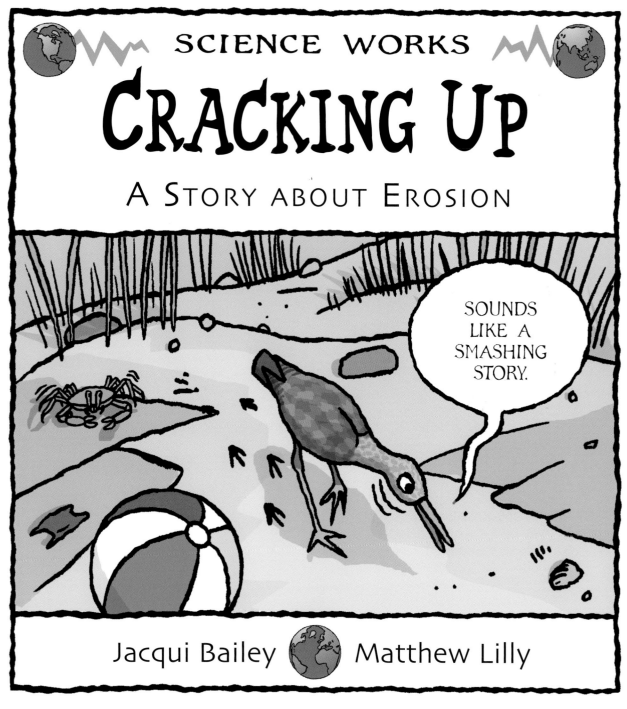

Picture Window Books • Minneapolis, Minnesota

Editor: Jacqueline A. Wolfe
Page Production: Melissa Kes
Creative Director: Keith Griffin
Editorial Director: Carol Jones

First American edition published in 2006 by
Picture Window Books
5115 Excelsior Boulevard
Suite 232
Minneapolis, MN 55416
1-877-845-8392
www.picturewindowbooks.com

First published in Great Britain by
A & C Black Publishers Limited
37 Soho Square, London W1D 3QZ
Copyright © Two's Company 2003

Printed in the United States of America.

Library of Congress Cataloging-in-Publication Data
Bailey, Jacqui.
Cracking up: a story about erosion / by Jacqui Bailey ; illustrated by Matthew Lilly.
p. cm. — (Science works)
Includes bibliographical references and index.
ISBN-13: 978-1-4048-1594-0 (hardcover)
ISBN-10: 1-4048-1594-5 (hardcover)
ISBN-13: 978-1-4048-1996-2 (paperback)
ISBN-10: 1-4048-1996-7 (paperback)
1. Erosion—Juvenile literature I. Lilly, Matthew, ill. II. Title.
QE571.B29 2006
551.3'02—dc22   2005030010

For Chris
JB

For Ben
ML

Special thanks to our advisers for their
expertise, research, and advice:

Larry M. Browning, Ph.D., Professor
Physics Department, South Dakota State University
Brookings, South Dakota, USA

Dr. Robin Armstrong, Peter Tandy,
and Charlotte Stockley
Mineralogy Department at the
Natural History Museum
London, England

Susan Kesselring, M.A., Literacy Educator
Rosemount-Apple Valley-Eagan
(Minnesota) School District

> With many thanks
> to geologist and science
> editor, Dr. Ted Nield.

3

The rocky ledge poked out from the cliff face, high above the sea.

A patch of short, stringy grass clung to it, and bird droppings streaked its sides.

The ledge had been there for a very long time.

It was there when the Roman Empire came and went.

It was there when knights built castles and fought battles.

It was still there when the first steam trains puffed across the land ...

... and the first aircrafts flew through the sky.

From the very beginning, erosion was taking place on the cliff.

Every spring, seagulls built nests on the ledge ...

... laid their eggs, and raised their young.

In summer, the hot sun baked the cliff face. The tufts of grass turned brown and dusty, and the rock was warm to touch.

HMMM, THAT'S A HANDY-LOOKING LEDGE.

MOVE OVER!

Sometimes sea birds pecked and scraped at the ledge as they fought for space to perch. Their claws and beaks left little scratches and grooves in the rock.

6

Each autumn, most of the birds flew off to warmer places. Strong winds blew in from the sea and beat against the cliff face. The wind carried specks of dust and grit that rubbed the ledge like sandpaper.

BRRR! IT'S TIME TO GO.

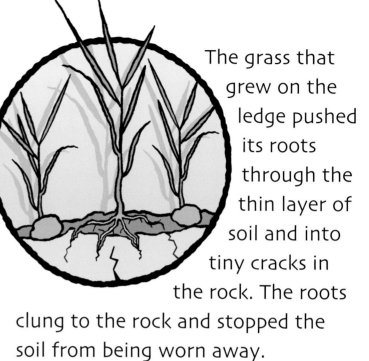

The grass that grew on the ledge pushed its roots through the thin layer of soil and into tiny cracks in the rock. The roots clung to the rock and stopped the soil from being worn away.

Soil is made from tiny powdery pieces of rock mixed with bits of dead plants and animals. Over thousands of years, rainwater crumbles rock into dust and this builds up on the land as soil. Without soil, plants could not grow. Plants help slow erosion.

7

In winter, the days were cold and wet. Rainwater soaked into every crack and hole in the cliff.

IT'S FREEZING OUT HERE!

It grew so cold that the rain turned to snow and the water in the cracks froze into ice. The ice made the cracks wider. When the ice melted, the cracks filled up with more water than before.

As water freezes into ice, it expands (swells up) so the ice takes up more space. The expanding ice is very strong. When water freezes inside the cracks in rock, the ice is powerful enough to push the rock apart. This makes the cracks bigger and can break the rock into pieces.

Below the ledge, the seawater rose and fell. Waves crashed against the foot of the cliff, gradually undercutting it.

Each year, the ledge seemed to stick out more because the cliff under it was eroding away. The sun, wind, and rain wore deep grooves into the sides of the ledge. Its edges began to crumble.

Water is heavy. When a large wave hits something, it can have as much force as a speeding car. As each wave hits the base of the cliff, it thrusts water into every gap and crack. The cracks slowly widen until chunks of rock fall away. Over time, the base of the cliff is eroded away.

AWWK! MAYBE I WON'T LAND HERE AFTER ALL.

Bit by bit, the ledge was being worn away. It was being eroded.

Erosion is the name scientists give to the way in which water, ice, wind, and sun wear away at Earth's surface and change the shape of the land.

Earth's surface is made of rock. On land the rock is usually covered with a layer of soil, but you can see bare rock in cliffs and on mountainsides, where there is no soil or where the soil is very thin.

solid rock

We think of rock as hard and solid, but over hundreds or thousands of years, ice and rainwater wear down mountains.

Rivers cut deep valleys into the land.

Hot days and cold nights bake and shatter desert cliffs. Dusty winds scrub against rocks and boulders and erode them into strange shapes.

PHEW, I'M BAKING!

Ocean waves erode the land's edges.

Plants help break up rocks, too. Plant roots push their way into cracks in the rock. As the roots grow, they make the cracks wider. Then water can get into the rock and make it crumble.

One winter there was a great storm. Wind and rain lashed at the cliff, and the waves rose higher and higher.

Waves are made by wind blowing across the surface of the sea. The size of the waves depends on the strength of the wind.

UH, OH . . .

LOOK OUT!

The ledge split away from the cliff and toppled into the sea. As it fell, it broke into pieces which sank to the seabed.

There was a creaking, groaning sound and then a loud ...

C R A C K !

But the waves didn't let the pieces of ledge stay there. The water heaved and rolled and crashed the pieces on the seabed. This broke them up even more. The cliff was being eroded away.

Waves don't only happen on the surface of the water. Underneath the waves, the water is churning around and around, a bit like the water in a washing machine.

The storm died away and the sea grew calmer, but the waves still rolled in. Each wave brought a surge of water that tumbled the pieces of rock forward, then sucked them back as the water flowed away again. The underwater waves were eroding the cliff.

LOOK! NEW ROCKS TO PLAY WITH!

The pieces of ledge rolled backward and forward, backward and forward, until their edges were worn smooth. They no longer looked like chunks of broken ledge, but like lumpy rocks. Some were the size of bricks.

I'M SURE THESE ROCKS USED TO BE BIGGER.

Day after day, the tides came and went. When the seas were rough and stormy, big waves lifted up the rocks and threw them against the cliff, helping to erode it even more.

WHOA!

CRASH!

BASH!

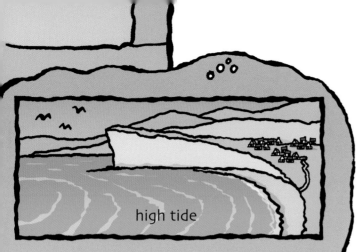

high tide

Twice a day, the sea rises higher up the coast than at other times. This rise and fall in the level of the sea is called the tide. When the tide reaches its highest point, it starts to shrink back. When it reaches its lowest point, it starts to rise again.

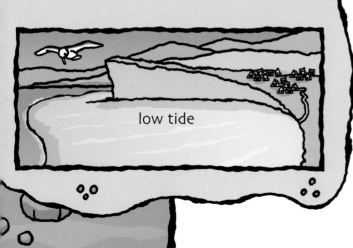

low tide

Some of the rocks were smashed into smaller, pebble-sized pieces.

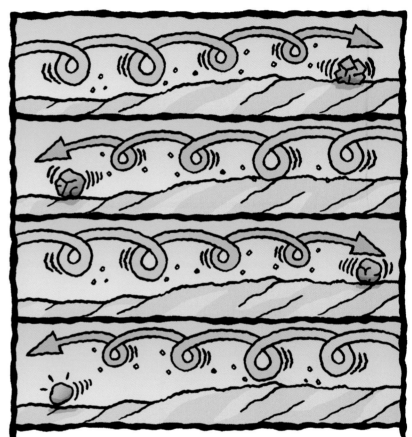

Then their sharp broken edges were slowly ground smooth again as they rolled backward and forward and backward and forward in the sea.

All this rolling around wore the pebbles away, but something else was happening to them, too. Little by little, the water was dissolving them.

Rock is made of lots of pieces of stuff called minerals. Some minerals dissolve in water and are washed away, leaving tiny holes in the surface of the rock. The holes also make the surface of the rock weaker so that it is more easily worn away.

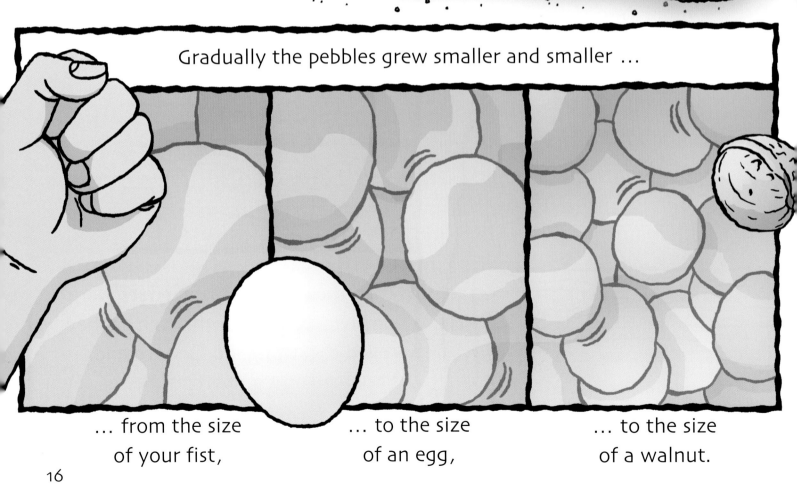

Gradually the pebbles grew smaller and smaller …

… from the size of your fist,

… to the size of an egg,

… to the size of a walnut.

Now when the waves lifted them up, the pebbles were so small and light that they hung in the water for a little while before sinking back to the seabed.

When the next wave came, the water pushed the small pebbles sideways. The pebbles gradually began to drift around the side of the cliff.

IT'S A GOOD DAY FOR FLYING.

The side of the cliff curved back from the sea into a wide bay with a sandy beach. Slowly, the pebbles were being carried toward the bay.

Some types of rock are softer than others and are eroded more quickly. When soft rock lies between hard rock, the sea carves away the soft rock much faster, and a bay is formed. The hard rock is left sticking out on either side of the bay.

The water in the bay was calmer than at the foot of the cliff. Here, the waves rolled all the way onto the shore.

The seabed was different, too. Instead of big boulders and piles of rock, it was covered with sand, pebbles, and the empty shells of dead sea creatures—with just a few large rocks scattered around.

Seaweed and shellfish clung to the rocks, and crabs, lobsters, and fish darted through the water or searched among the pebbles for scraps of food.

As each wave rolled toward the shore, it picked up small pebbles and grains of sand and washed them closer and closer to the beach.

The pebbles from our ledge were carried along with the rest. As they traveled, they rubbed and rolled against the sand, stones, and shells on the seabed until the pebbles were no bigger than the size of your little fingernail.

Little by little, the pebbles moved closer to the shore.

One windy day, when the waves were big and fierce, the pebbles were lifted high and flung up onto the beach.

This time, when the tide went out it left the pebbles behind, gleaming in the sun. By now, the pebbles were so small they were the size of grains of rice. They had become grains of sand.

HEY, WE'VE BEEN LEFT BEHIND!

Where the seabed slopes up toward the shore, the water gets shallower. In shallow water, the tops of the waves curve over and crash down in a mass of white foam called surf.

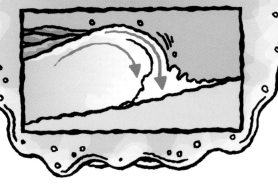

Sometimes the wind or the tides moved the grains of sand along the beach.

Sometimes shore crabs scuttled over them, or shore birds pecked at them in search of sandworms.

In summer, lots of people visited the beach and walked or played on the sand.

One day, a child scooped up the sand and pushed it into a bucket. She pressed it down firmly with her shovel.

She turned the bucket over and patted its base. When she lifted the bucket away, she had made a sand castle.

Because of erosion, the grains of sand were high above the ground like they were on the cliff—at least, until the next tide came in.

23

SEAS OF SAND

Beaches aren't the only places with lots of sand. Deserts may be far from the coast, yet some contain vast seas of sand. The sand is made by erosion caused by the sun and wind.

Deserts have almost no rain, so there are few plants and little soil to cover the rocks. Sandy deserts are baking hot in the daytime but cold at night. The change from hot to cold to hot again cracks surface rocks apart. Dusty winds rub against rocks, gradually grinding them into sand. Over thousands of years, the sand builds into flowing heaps called sand dunes.

SAVING SOIL

Without erosion, we wouldn't have any soil. Erosion breaks down rock into dust and clay, which mix with bits of rotting plants and animals to make soil. But erosion can destroy soil, too. Soil takes thousands of years to make, but it can be blown away by wind or washed away by water in just a few months.

Plant roots, especially tree roots, help to hold down soil and to protect it. In some places, people have cut down lots of trees to make way for farmland. But when the soil is left bare, rain and wind erode it away, leaving the land useless.

IT IS POSSIBLE TO HAVE TOO MUCH SAND.

NEW FOR OLD

With all this erosion going on, you might think there would be no solid rocks left on Earth. But erosion is often a very slow process. Some rock can take millions of years to erode, and while it is wearing away, new rock is being made.

New rock comes from deep inside Earth. It bursts out as hot, liquid rock from volcanoes and from huge cracks in the seabed. When the liquid rock cools, it hardens into layers of solid rock. Most new rock is found on the seabed.

NEW ROCK DELIVERY!

ROCK SANDWICHES

Not all rock is new rock. A lot of the rock we see on land is recycled. Sand and dust build up in thick layers at the bottom of seas and lakes. These layers get heavier and heavier as the ones on top press down on those at the bottom. Eventually, the bottom layers are squeezed so hard they turn back into solid rock.

Millions of years later, as the surface of Earth slowly changes, these layers of rock may be pushed back up to the surface again as cliffs or mountains.

TRY IT AND SEE

EXPANDING ICE

When water freezes it has the power to push rocks apart.

Try this experiment to discover the strength of expanding ice.

You will need:
- A plastic glass
- Some water
- A plate that fits on top of the glass
- A large pebble or other weight

 Put the weight on top of the plate and carefully put the whole thing in the freezer overnight.

 When you take it out of the freezer you should see that the ice has lifted the plate and the weight above the rim of the glass.

1 Fill the glass with as much water as you can and place the plate on top.

26

ICE ATTACK

Cold nights and warmer days can freeze and thaw rocks over and over again.

See how these changes of temperature help to erode rocks.

You will need:
- Modeling clay
- A water spray bottle
- Plastic wrap
- A plate

1 Divide the clay in two and roll each piece into a ball.

2 Spray both the clay balls with water and wrap them up in plastic wrap.

3 Leave one on a plate, and put the other one in the freezer overnight.

4 In the morning, take out the frozen ball and let it thaw out. Then, unwrap the plastic wrap and compare the two balls of clay. The one you froze should have some small cracks on its surface. If you keep spraying, freezing, and thawing it, the cracks in the clay will get bigger and bigger. This is what happens to rocks.

CRACKING FACTS

When sand is heated to more than 2192 °F (1200 °C) it melts into a clear liquid. When the liquid cools it hardens into glass. Glass-blowers make beautiful shapes with glass by dipping a long tube into the hot liquid and blowing down the tube into the blob of glass at the end.

MMMM, NOW THIS IS WHAT I CALL A TASTY PIECE OF ROCK.

You often see patches of crusty-looking green or yellow plant-like stuff growing on rocks. These are lichens (*lie-kens*). Lichens don't need soil to grow—they can live on bare rock. They make a liquid that slowly seeps into the rock and dissolves it so the lichens can suck up minerals from the rock. This weakens the rock and it erodes more quickly.

YOO HOO, IS ANYBODY THERE?

Erosion doesn't only happen on Earth's surface. Rainwater soaks through soil into the rocks below. Some rocks, such as limestone, dissolve in water—just like sugar dissolves in water, only much more slowly. The water gradually wears away at the rock. Over thousands of years, the cracks become holes, caves, and huge caverns, hidden deep underground.

28

GLOSSARY

desert—a dry place that gets very little rain

erosion—when soil is worn away by water, wind, ice, and the sun.

pebble—a small, usually rounded stone that has been worn by the action of water

tide—the rising and falling of the ocean over the shore; usually the tide rises and falls twice a day

valley—a low point of Earth's surface, between ranges of hills or mountains

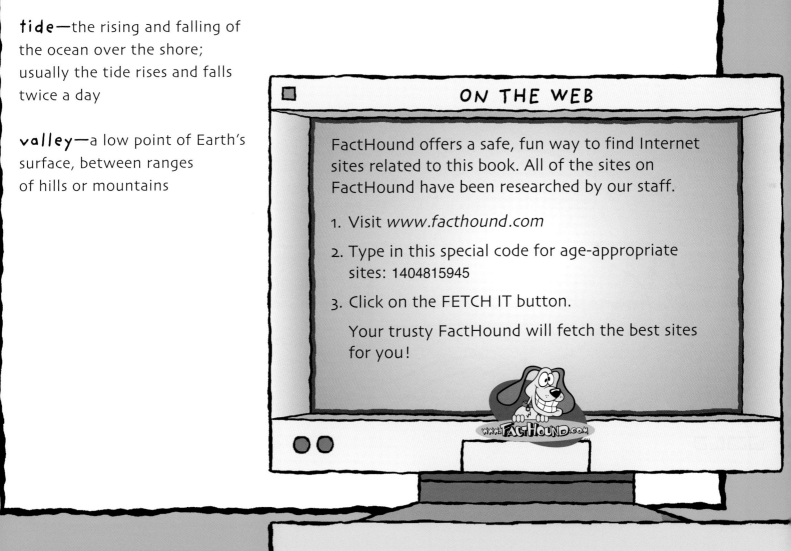

ON THE WEB

FactHound offers a safe, fun way to find Internet sites related to this book. All of the sites on FactHound have been researched by our staff.

1. Visit *www.facthound.com*

2. Type in this special code for age-appropriate sites: 1404815945

3. Click on the FETCH IT button.

   Your trusty FactHound will fetch the best sites for you!

www.FactHound.com

INDEX

bays, 18, 19
beach animals, 22
beaches, 18, 20, 21, 22, 23
caves, 28
deserts, 11, 24
erosion, 6, 7, 9, 10–11, 13, 14, 19, 24, 25, 27, 28
ice, 8, 10, 11, 26, 27
lichens, 28
minerals, 16, 28
mountains, 10, 11, 25
pebbles, 15, 16, 17, 18, 19, 20, 21
plants, 7, 11, 24

rainwater, 7, 8, 9, 11, 12, 24, 28
rivers, 11
rocks, 6, 7, 8, 9, 10, 11, 13, 14, 15, 16, 19, 24, 25, 26, 27, 28
dissolving rock, 16, 28
roots, 7, 11, 24
sand, 19, 20, 21, 22, 23, 24, 25, 28
seabed, 12, 13, 17, 19, 20, 21, 25
sea creatures, 19
seagulls, 6
seaweed, 19

shells, 19, 20
snow, 8
soil, 7, 10, 24, 28
sun, 6, 9, 10, 21, 24
surf, 21
tides, 14, 15, 21, 22, 23
undercutting, 9
valleys, 11
volcanoes, 25
water, 8, 9, 10, 11, 13, 16, 17, 19, 21, 24, 26, 28
waves, 9, 11, 12, 13, 14, 17, 19, 20, 21
wind, 7, 9, 10, 11, 12, 21, 22, 24

Read all of the books in the Science Works series:

A Drop in the Ocean:
The Story of Water
1-4048-0566-4

Charged Up:
The Story of Electricity
1-4048-0568-0

Cracking Up:
A Story About Erosion
1-4048-1594-5

Monster Bones :
The Story of a Dinosaur Fossil
1-4048-0565-6

The Rock Factory:
A Story of Rocks and Stones
1-4048-1596-1

Staying Alive:
The Story of a Food Chain
1-4048-1595-3

Sun Up, Sun Down:
The Story of Day and Night
1-4048-0567-2

Up, Down, All Around:
A Story of Gravity
1-4048-1597-X